The Tet Offensive: The History and Legacy of the Most Famous Military Campaign of the Vietnam War

By Charles River Editors

Viet Cong troops posing with American weaponry and radios

About Charles River Editors

Charles River Editors provides superior editing and original writing services across the digital publishing industry, with the expertise to create digital content for publishers across a vast range of subject matter. In addition to providing original digital content for third party publishers, we also republish civilization's greatest literary works, bringing them to new generations of readers via ebooks.

Sign up here to receive updates about free books as we publish them, and visit Our Kindle Author Page to browse today's free promotions and our most recently published Kindle titles.

Introduction

Residents fleeing the Battle of Quang Tri

The Tet Offensive

"This spring far outshines the previous springs,

Of triumphs throughout the land come happy tidings.

Let North and South emulate each other in fighting the U. S. aggressors!

Forward! Total victory will be ours." - Ho Chi Minh on Radio Hanoi, January 1 1968

"We have been too often disappointed by the optimism of the American leaders, both in Vietnam and Washington, to have faith any longer in the silver linings they find in the darkest clouds…we are mired in a stalemate that could only be ended by negotiation, not victory." – Walter Cronkite, February 27, 1968

The Vietnam War could have been called a comedy of errors if the consequences weren't so deadly and tragic. In 1951, while war was raging in Korea, the United States began signing defense pacts with nations in the Pacific, intending to create alliances that would contain the spread of Communism. As the Korean War was winding down, America joined the Southeast Asia Treaty Organization, pledging to defend several nations in the region from Communist aggression. One of those nations was South Vietnam.

Before the Vietnam War, most Americans would have been hard pressed to locate Vietnam on a map. South Vietnamese President Diem's regime was extremely unpopular, and war broke out between Communist North Vietnam and South Vietnam around the end of the 1950s. Kennedy's administration tried to prop up the South Vietnamese with training and assistance, but the South Vietnamese military was feeble. A month before his death, Kennedy signed a presidential directive withdrawing 1,000 American personnel, and shortly after Kennedy's assassination, new President Lyndon B. Johnson reversed course, instead opting to expand American assistance to South Vietnam.

Over the next few years, the American military commitment to South Vietnam grew dramatically, and the war effort became both deeper and more complex. The strategy included parallel efforts to strengthen the economic and political foundations of the South Vietnamese regime, to root out the Viet Cong guerrilla insurgency in the south, combat the more conventional North Vietnamese Army (NVA) near the Demilitarized Zone between north and south, and bomb military and industrial targets in North Vietnam itself. In public, American military officials and members of the Johnson administration stressed their tactical successes and offered rosy predictions; speaking before the National Press Club in November 1967, General Westmoreland claimed, ""I have never been more encouraged in the four years that I have been in Vietnam. We are making real progress...I am absolutely certain that whereas in 1965 the enemy was winning, today he is certainly losing." (*New York Times*, November 22, 1967).

At the same time, the government worked to conceal from the American public their own doubts and the grim realities of war. Reflecting on the willful public optimism of American officials at the time, Colonel Harry G. Summers concluded, "We in the military knew better, but through fear of reinforcing the basic antimilitarism of the American people we tended to keep this knowledge to ourselves and downplayed battlefield realities . . . We had concealed from the American people the true nature of the war." (Summers, 63).

By the end of 1967, with nearly half a million troops deployed, more than 19,000 deaths, and a war that cost $2 billion a month and seemed to grow bloodier by the day, the Johnson administration faced an increasingly impatient and skeptical nation. Early in 1968, a massive coordinated Viet Cong operation - the Tet Offensive - briefly paralyzed American and South Vietnamese forces across the country, threatening even the American embassy compound in Saigon. With this, the smiling mask slipped even further, inflaming the burgeoning antiwar movement. Although American soldiers didn't lose a battle strategically during the campaign, the Tet Offensive made President Johnson non-credible and historically unpopular, to the extent that he did not run for reelection in 1968. By then, Vietnam had already fueled the hippie counterculture, and anti-war protests spread across the country. On campuses and in the streets, some protesters spread peace and love, but others rioted. In August 1968, riots broke out in the streets of Chicago, as the National Guard and police took on 10,000 anti-war rioters during the Democratic National Convention. By the end of the decade, Vietnam had left tens of thousands of Americans dead, spawned a counterculture with millions of protesters, and destroyed a presidency, and more was still yet to come.

Nearly 50 years after the campaign, the Tet Offensive continues to inspire impassioned and occasionally bitter debate among historians, military officers, government officials, veterans, journalists, and the public at large. Was the large-scale Communist assault a strategic masterstroke that demolished American popular support for the war effort? Was it a catastrophic misstep that effectively broke the back of the Viet Cong guerrilla forces in South Vietnam? Did Tet expose the Johnson administration's optimistic pronouncements as a deliberate pattern of lies and obfuscations designed to mislead the American public about the true nature of the war? Or did anti-war elements in the news media betray their public trust by mischaracterizing a substantial American victory as a shocking and catastrophic defeat? In the words of the historian Richard Falk, the Tet Offensive "remains a mirror for restating opposed preconceptions and validating contending ideological biases." (Falk, 11). Perhaps the only proposition to win universal agreement is that the Tet Offensive represented a significant turning point. The conflict in Vietnam would continue for years after Tet, but it would never be the same.

The Tet Offensive: The History and Legacy of the Most Famous Military Campaign of the Vietnam War chronicles one of the largest campaigns of the war and the effects it had on both sides. Along with pictures of important people, places, and events, you will learn about the Tet Offensive like never before, in no time at all.

The Tet Offensive: The History and Legacy of the Most Famous Military Campaign of the Vietnam War

About Charles River Editors

Introduction

Chapter 1: Historical Background

"The last thing I wanted to do was to be a wartime President." – Lyndon B. Johnson

By the start of 1968, the United States had been heavily invested in opposing Vietnamese communism for the better part of two decades, and with the benefit of hindsight, the American war effort that metastasized there throughout the 1960s may seem like a grievous error and a needless waste of blood and treasure on an unwinnable and strategically insignificant civil conflict in a distant, culturally alien land. Indeed, it is still difficult for Americans today to comprehend how it was that their leaders determined such a course was in the national interest. Thus, it is essential at the outset to inquire how it was that a succession of elite American politicians, bureaucrats, and military officers managed, often despite their own inherent skepticism, to convince both themselves and the public that a communist Vietnam would constitute a grave threat to America's security.

Vietnam's first modern revolution came in the months of violence, famine, and chaos that succeeded World War II in Asia. Along with present-day Laos and Cambodia, the country had been a French colony since the late 19th century, but more recently, at the outset of World War II, the entire region had been occupied by the Japanese. Despite the pan-Asian anti-colonialism they publicly espoused, Japan did little to alter the basic structures of political and economic control the French had erected.

When Japan surrendered and relinquished all claim to its overseas empire, spontaneous uprisings occurred in Hanoi, Hue, and other Vietnamese cities. These were seized upon by the Vietnam Independence League (or *Vietminh*) and its iconic leader Ho Chi Minh, who declared an independent Democratic Republic of Vietnam (DRV) on September 2, 1945. France, which had reoccupied most of the country by early 1946, agreed in theory to grant the DRV limited autonomy. However, when the sharp limits of that autonomy became apparent, the Vietminh took up arms. By the end of 1946, in the first instance of what would become a longstanding pattern, the French managed to retain control of the cities while the rebels held sway in the countryside.

Ho Chi Minh

From the outset, Ho hoped to avoid conflict with the United States. He was a deeply committed Communist and dedicated to class warfare and social revolution, but at the same time, he was also a steadfast Vietnamese nationalist who remained wary of becoming a puppet of the Soviet Union or the People's Republic of China. Indeed, Ho's very real popularity throughout the country rested to no small extent on his ability to tap into a centuries-old popular tradition of national resistance against powerful foreign hegemons, a tradition originally directed against imperial China. As such, he made early advances to Washington, even deliberately echoing the American Declaration of Independence in his own declaration of Vietnamese independence.

Under different circumstances, Americans might not have objected much to a communist but independent DRV. The Roosevelt and Truman administrations had trumpeted national independence in Asia and exhibited almost nothing but contempt for French colonial rule. However, as Cold War tensions rose, and as the Soviet Union and (after 1949) Communist China increased their material and rhetorical support for the Vietminh cause, such subtle gradations quickly faded. Considering the matter in May 1949, Secretary of State Dean Acheson asserted that the question of whether Ho was "as much nationalist as Commie is irrelevant. All Stalinists in colonial areas are nationalists . . . Once in power their objective necessarily becomes subordination [of the] state to Commie purpose." (Young, 20 – 23).

Acheson

As a result, in 1950, the United States recognized the new puppet government France had established under the emperor Bao Dai, and by 1953 American financial aid funded fully 60% of France's counterinsurgency effort. When that effort finally collapsed in 1954, an international conference at Geneva agreed to divide Vietnam at the 17th parallel into a communist DRV in the north and an American-backed Republic of Vietnam in the south. Between 1955 and 1961, South Vietnam and its new president, Ngo Dinh Diem, received more than $1 billion in American aid. Even so, Diem proved unable to consolidate support for his regime, and by 1961 he faced a growing insurgency in the Viet Cong (VC), a coalition of local guerrilla groups supported and directed by North Vietnam.

Diem

Bao Dai

As Diem and (after a 1963 coup) his successors teetered on the brink of disaster, American politicians and military officers grappled with the difficult question of how much they were willing to sacrifice to support an ally. In 1961, President Kennedy resisted a push to mount air strikes, but he agreed to send increased financial aid to South Vietnam, along with hundreds (and eventually thousands) of American "military advisors."

The summer of 1964, which would normally be used to prepare for reelection, was a busy time for Lyndon B. Johnson's Administration. His attempts to steamroll ahead on domestic policy legislation were quickly sideswiped by a surprising foreign policy event: the Gulf of Tonkin incident. In 1964, the *USS Maddox* was an intelligence-gathering naval ship stationed off the coast of North Vietnam for the purpose of gathering information about the ongoing conflict between North Vietnam and South Vietnam. The borders between North and South, however, were in dispute, and the United States was less up to date on changes in these borders than the two belligerents. In the process, the *USS Maddox* accidentally crossed over into North Vietnamese shores, and when the ship was sighted by North Vietnamese naval units, they attacked the *Maddox* on August 2, 1964.

Though no Americans were hurt, naval crews were on heightened alert as the *Maddox* retreated to South Vietnam, where it was met by the USS *Turner Joy*. Two days later, the *Maddox* and *Turner Joy*, both with crews already on edge as a result of the events of August 2, were certain they were being followed by hostile North Vietnamese boats, and both fired at targets popping up on their radar.

After this second encounter, Johnson gave a speech over radio to the American people shortly before midnight on August 4th. He told of attacks on the high seas, suggesting the events occurred in international waters, and vowed the nation would be prepared for its own defense and the defense of the South Vietnamese. Johnson thus had the Gulf of Tonkin Resolution drafted, which gave the right of military preparedness to the President without Congressional approval. The resolution passed shortly thereafter, giving the President the authority to raise military units in Vietnam and engage in warfare as needed without any consent from Congress. Shortly thereafter, President Johnson approved air strikes against the North Vietnamese, and Congress approved military action with the Gulf of Tonkin Resolution.

Once upon a time, Johnson had claimed, "We are not about to send American boys 9 or 10 thousand miles away from home to do what Asian boys ought to be doing for themselves." By the end of the year, however, over 16,000 Americans were stationed in South Vietnam. Regarding this about-face, Johnson would explain, "Just like the Alamo, somebody damn well needed to go to their aid. Well, by God, I'm going to Vietnam's aid!"

It would be years before the government revealed that the second encounter was no encounter at all. The government never figured out what the *Maddox* and *Turner Joy* were firing at that night, but there was no indication that it involved the North Vietnamese. Regardless, by 1965, under intense pressure from his advisors and with regular units of the NVA infiltrating into the south, President Lyndon Johnson reluctantly agreed to a bombing campaign, Operation Rolling Thunder, against North Vietnamese targets. He also agreed to a request from General William Westmoreland, the American military commander in South Vietnam, for the first American ground troops deployed to Vietnam: two battalions of Marines to guard the air bases.

Westmoreland

Years later, General Frederick Weyand speculated that the disingenuous pronouncements of officers and politicians, while instrumental in making the initial case for intervention, may have poisoned the well of long-term public support: "The American way of war is particularly violent, deadly and dreadful. We believe in using 'things'—artillery, bombs, massive firepower—in order to conserve our soldiers' lives. The enemy, on the other hand, made up for his lack of 'things' by expending men instead of machines, and he suffered enormous casualties. The army saw this happen in Korea, and we should have made the realities of war obvious to the American people before they witnessed it on their television screens. The army must make the price of involvement clear before we get involved." (Summers, 68).

Whether greater openness from the outset might have translated into steadier national resolve in the long term is impossible to say, but it would almost certainly have punctured some of the dangerous illusions that young American soldiers brought with them to Vietnam.

Compared with their predecessors in World War II and Korea, the average American soldier in Vietnam was considerably younger and in many cases came from more marginal economic backgrounds. The average American soldier in World War II was 26, but in Vietnam, the average soldier was barely 19. In part, this was due to President Johnson's refusal to mobilize the national reserves; concerned that calling up the National Guard would spook the public and possibly antagonize the Russians or Chinese, Johnson relied on the draft to fill the ranks of the military.

In all, between 1964 and 1973, fully 2.2 million American men were drafted into the military, and an additional 8.7 million enlisted voluntarily, or at least semi-voluntarily. Knowing that draftees were more likely to be assigned to combat roles, many men who expected to be drafted took the initiative to enlist in the military before the Selective Service Board had a chance to call them up. This was a risky bet, perhaps, but not necessarily a crazy one, because enlistees were less than half as likely as draftees to be killed in Vietnam.

Moreover, given the numerous Selective Service deferments available for attending college, being married, holding a defense-related job, or serving in the National Guard, the burden of the draft fell overwhelmingly on the people from working class backgrounds. It also particularly affected African Americans.

The American military that these young draftees and enlistees joined had been forged in the crucible of World War II and were tempered by two decades of Cold War with the Soviet Union. In terms of its organization, equipment, training regimens, operational doctrines, and its very outlook, the American military was designed to fight a major conventional war against a similarly-constituted force, whether in Western Europe or among the plains of northeast Asia. As an organization, the military's collective memories were of just such engagements at places like Midway, Normandy, Iwo Jima, Incheon, and the Battle of the Bulge. These campaigns predominately involved battles of infantry against infantry, tanks against tanks, and jet fighters against jet fighters. As boys, many of the young men who fought in Vietnam had played as soldiers, re-enacting the heroic tales of their fathers and grandfathers. The author Philip Caputo, who arrived in Vietnam as a young marine officer in 1965, recalled, "I saw myself charging up some distant beachhead, like John Wayne in *Sands of Iwo Jima*, and then coming home with medals on my chest." (Caputo, 6).

Expecting a simple conflict of good against evil and knowing little to nothing of the local culture, American soldiers in their late teens and early twenties arrived in Vietnam and found a world of peril, privation, and moral ambiguity. Despairing of and for young rookie soldiers like Caputo, Bruce Lawler, a CIA case officer in South Vietnam, virtually exploded with rage: "How in hell can you put people like that into a war? How can you inject these types of guys into a situation that requires a tremendous amount of sophistication? You can't. What happens is they start shooting at anything that moves because they don't know. They're scared. I mean, they're out there getting shot at, and Christ, there's somebody with eyes that are different from mine. And boom—it's gone." (Saltoli, 177).

Indeed, with a few notable exceptions, the American military experience in Vietnam consisted largely of small-scale encounters. Understanding full well that contesting a conventional battle with the better-armed Americans amounted to committing suicide, the Viet Cong waged an asymmetrical guerrilla-style campaign that capitalized on their superior knowledge of the terrain, their closer relations with local villagers, and their deeper commitment to the cause. Viet Cong guerrillas wore no uniforms, did not always bear their arms openly, did not observe traditional battle lines, and blended in with the villagers who supported them. During the war, an American soldier was as likely to be killed by a land mine, a booby trap, or a hidden sniper as by an enemy he could see.

To the Viet Cong themselves, such tactics were natural and justified in a "people's war": "The soldiers came from the people. They were the children of the villagers. The villagers loved them, protected them, fed them. They were the people's soldiers." (FitzGerald, 201). To the Americans, however, the insurgents seemed sneaky and treacherous, readier to hide behind women and children than to stand and fight like men.

Of course, such guerrilla tactics served to blur the lines between combatant and civilian. As Specialist 4th Class Fred Widmer of Charlie Company explained, "The same village you had gone in to give them medical treatment . . . you could go through that village later and get shot at on your way out by a sniper. Go back in, you wouldn't find anybody. Nobody knew anything . . . You didn't trust them anymore." (Widmer).

Faced with such a determined opponent, skilled in asymmetrical warfare and enjoying considerable popular support, General Westmoreland chose to fight a war of attrition. While he did employ strategic hamlets, pacification programs, and other kinetic counterinsurgency operations, he largely relied on his massive advantage in firepower to overwhelm and grind down the Viet Cong and NVA in South Vietnam. The goal was simple: to reach a "crossover point" at which communist fighters were being killed more quickly than they could be replaced. American ground forces would lure the enemy into the open, where they would be destroyed by a combination of artillery and air strikes.

Naturally, if American soldiers on the ground often had trouble distinguishing combatants from civilians, B-52 bombers flying at up to 30,000 feet were wholly indiscriminate when targeting entire villages. By the end of 1966, American bombers and fighter-bombers in Vietnam dropped about 825 tons of explosive every day, more than all the bombs dropped on Europe during World War II. As Secretary of Defense Robert McNamara wrote to President Johnson in May of 1967, "The picture of the world's greatest superpower killing or seriously injuring 1,000 noncombatants a week, while trying to pound a tiny backward nation into submission on an issue whose merits are hotly disputed, is not a pretty one." (Sheehan, 685).

By 1968, civilian casualties in South Vietnam were estimated to be at least 300,000 per year, and Westmoreland has often been criticized for employing such a brutal and ultimately ineffective strategy. In fairness, however, it must be noted that he had few genuinely attractive options. Seeking out a decisive victory by invading the north had been ruled out by the Johnson administration as too provocative since it was likely to pull China or the Soviet Union into the war, but Westmoreland's troops were too few, too young, and too inexperienced to carry out a full counterinsurgency as the British had in Malaya. As Westmoreland later argued, "Had I at my disposal virtually unlimited manpower, I could have stationed troops permanently in every district or province and thus provided an alternative strategy. That would have enabled the troops to get to know the people intimately, facilitating the task of identifying the subversives and protecting the others against intimidation. Yet to have done that would have required literally millions of men." (Westmoreland).

This may well be so, but it is difficult to deny that the strategy of attrition - and the largely indiscriminate means used to achieve it - were bound to drive a wedge between the American military and even anti-communist civilians. "Search and destroy" missions sought to eliminate not only VC guerrillas but also any food, shelter, or materials they might use. Westmoreland and the Military Assistance Command, Vietnam (MACV) declared large swathes of South Vietnam as "free fire" zones, meaning villages in these zones could be carpet bombed and civilians were automatically considered enemy combatants.

Above all, success was measured in terms of "body count;" Westmoreland's staff estimated the crossover point at a kill ratio of 10 Viet Cong to every American. To that end, officers rewarded soldiers for confirmed kills, rules of engagement were unofficially loosened, and operations were sometimes planned solely to increase the body count. As Philip Caputo notes, the consequences of such a strategy for the outlook of the ordinary American soldier were as tragic as they were predictable: "General Westmoreland's strategy of attrition also had an important effect on our behavior. Our mission was not to win terrain or seize positions, but simply to kill: to kill Communists and to kill as many of them as possible. Stack 'em like cordwood. Victory was a high body count, defeat a low kill ratio, war a matter of arithmetic. The pressure on unit commanders to produce enemy corpses was intense, and they in turn communicated it to their troops . . . It is not surprising, therefore, that some men acquired a contempt for human life and a predilection for taking it." (Caputo, xix).

Chapter 2: The Plan

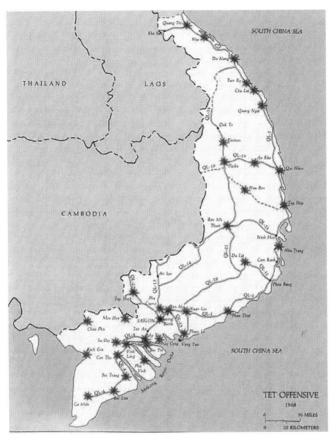

A map of targets for the Tet Offensive

The apparent stalemate of 1967 was not only a concern for the Americans. In Hanoi, Ho Chi Minh's war council debated its own strategy for driving the Americans and their allies from the south. In 1966, the party had agreed to pursue "decisive victory in a relatively short time." (Duiker, 263). However, their aggressive battlefield operations over the succeeding year - combined actions of both southern Viet Cong guerrilla cadres and units of the North Vietnamese Army spirited south along the Ho Chi Minh Trail - proved largely ineffective against the combined forces of the South Vietnamese Army and the increasing numbers of American troops in the Military Assistance Command, Vietnam (MACV). In the words of one Communist general, "In the spring of 1967 [MACV commander General William] Westmoreland began his second campaign. It was very fierce. Certain of our people were very discouraged. There was much discussion of the war—should we continue main-force efforts or should we pull back into a more local strategy. But by the middle of 1967 we concluded that [the Americans and South Vietnamese] had not reversed the balance of forces on the battlefield. So we decided to carry out one decisive battle to force LBJ to de-escalate the war." (Arnold, 9)

Two early, and persuasive, advocates of this strategy were Le Duan, Secretary General of the Lao Dong (Vietnam Workers' Party), and General Nguyen Chi Thanh, head of the NVA's Central Office for South Vietnam. Le Duan excoriated his more cautious comrades, arguing that a surprise mass offensive could strike the Americans and South Vietnamese at their weakest points: lukewarm public opinion in the United States and poor morale and readiness within the South Vietnamese military establishment. Thanh echoed these sentiments, contending that a mass assault on South Vietnamese cities and towns could set off a popular uprising among discontented South Vietnamese civilians.

Le Duan

Nguyen Chi Thanh

Interestingly, North Vietnam's Defense Minister, Vo Nguyen Giap, who would ultimately orchestrate the Tet Offensive and is often credited with originating it, actually opposed Le Duan and Thanh's proposal. Giap supported a protracted guerrilla struggle aimed at the Americans' supply and communications lines. He worried that such a large set-piece offensive would be bound to collapse in the face of superior American firepower, and that any such failure would severely curtail the war effort. Thanh mocked Giap as old-fashioned and overly cautious, a strategist with "a method of viewing things that is detached from reality," seeking answers "in books, and [by] mechanically copying one's past experiences or the experiences of foreign countries . . . in accordance with a dogmatic tendency." (Currey, 262 – 63).

Giap

In April 1967, after considerable debate, Thanh and Le Duan won the day when the 13th Plenum voted in favor of Resolution 13, a mass offensive combined with a "spontaneous uprising in order to win a decisive victory in the shortest possible time." (Gilbert and Head, 82). As it happened, however, Thanh did not live to see the culmination of his advocacy, dying of a heart attack in July 1967. With that, responsibility for planning and directing the Tet Offensive passed to Giap, who acceded to the collective will despite his personal reservations.

As the plan developed under Giap's leadership, the Tet Offensive would have three primary goals: to destroy the South Vietnamese military; to inspire a general uprising among South Vietnamese civilians; and to convince the American public that continued war in Vietnam was not worth the price. In the words of General Tran Van Tra, Commander of NVA forces in the south, the Viet Cong aimed "to break down and destroy the bulk of the puppet [South Vietnamese] troops, topple the puppet administration at all levels, and take power into the hands of the people; to destroy the major part of the U.S. forces and their war materiel, and render them unable to fulfill their political and military duties in Vietnam; and to break the U.S. will of aggression, force it to accept defeat in the South and put an end to all acts of war against the north." (Werner and Huynh, 40).

Tra

It is worth noting just how closely and thoroughly political and military goals intertwine in this statement. Here were the fingerprints of Giap, who would later explain, "For us, you know, there is no such thing as a single strategy. Ours is always a synthesis, simultaneously military, political, and diplomatic – which is why, quite clearly, the Tet Offensive had multiple objectives." (Karnow, 548). For Giap, the overarching goals of the Tet Offensive were never strictly military; he understood, certainly better than Thanh or Le Duan, that in a strictly military contest, the North Vietnamese cause was doomed. Instead, Giap saw military action as a means of transforming popular attitudes in both South Vietnam and the United States.

To achieve these ends, Giap insisted that the operation capitalize on both unprecedented reach and unprecedented shock. Thus, during the offensive, combined NVA and VC units would carry out an audacious wave of surprise attacks on cities and military bases not just in areas near the northern border, but throughout the entire South. With previously unthreatened urban centers like Saigon, Nha Trang, Qui Nhon, Quang Ngai, and Hue suddenly under siege, the veneer of American competence and control would be ripped away, and all Southern Vietnamese, including government officials, military officers, soldiers, and especially civilians, would be forced to conclude that nowhere was truly beyond the reach of the Viet Cong.

Chapter 3: The Diversion

Launching the offensive during the Tet holiday period, during which both sides had previously observed unofficial ceasefires and significant numbers of Southern soldiers and policemen would be on leave in their home villages, would ensure that the attacks caught the South Vietnamese military understaffed and off-guard. In fact, the endemic travel and bustle of the season would serve to mask the rivers of men and materiel pouring into position. As a result, in the weeks leading up to Tet, VC operatives smuggled weapons and ammunition to the outskirts of Southern cities in baskets of rice, beneath truckloads of fruits, vegetables, and flowers, and sometimes even in coffins. Northern troops disguised as civilians (or even as Southern soldiers) dissolved into the sea of pilgrims returning to their family homes for the New Year.

Not content to rely solely on these passive surprise measures, Giap orchestrated an elaborate "preparatory phase" to the Tet Offensive. From September-December 1967, Northern units struck repeatedly against remote outposts in the hilly regions along South Vietnam's Laotian and Cambodian borders, a large-scale feint designed to lure American and South Vietnamese forces west and away from the densely-populated central cities and towns that would be the ultimate targets of the offensive. In addition to muddying the strategic waters, these border strikes helped to distract American attention away from the men and equipment infiltrating south, while providing a chance for NVA and VC troops to rehearse the urban street-fighting tactics that would feature so heavily in the main offensive.

The first strike, which in a very real sense could be considered the first action of the Tet Offensive, came in July 1967 when NVA forces assaulted Con Thien, a Marine base at the extreme northeast corner of South Vietnam. For over three months, the battalion of Marines stationed there weathered both ground and artillery assaults. Finally, in the face of the Americans' massive air superiority (up to 790 B-52 sorties flown), the NVA were forced to lift the siege and withdraw on October 31.

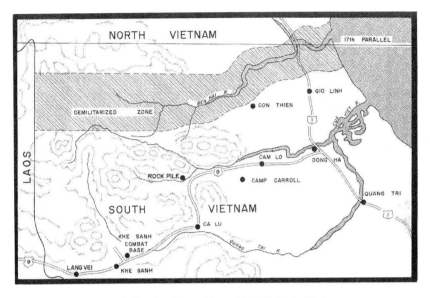

A map indicating the position of Con Thien in Vietnam

As it turned out, Con Thien was merely the first in a series of border strikes. On October 27, a South Vietnamese battalion in Song Be, near the Cambodian border, came under attack from an NVA regiment, and on October 29, a Viet Cong regiment struck a South Vietnamese base at Loc Ninh, further south and west along the border. Finally, November 17 saw the opening shots in a major confrontation between nine American and six NVA battalions over control of a U.S. Special Forces camp near Dak To in the central highlands along the Laotian border. These actions all followed a common pattern: a blistering surprise attack followed by intense fighting with high casualties on both sides, ending only when the overwhelming firepower (particularly the airpower) of the Americans and SVA succeeded in pushing the Communists back.

During the border strikes, American officers frequently expressed surprise at the grim tenacity with which NVA and VC troops help their positions. Standard practice prior to the Tet Offensive had been to strike quickly, do maximum damage, and then disappear into the jungle before the South Vietnamese or Americans could respond in full force. At Con Thien, Song Be, Loc Ninh, and Dak To, however, the North Vietnamese used new tactics designed to take and hold territory, tactics that would be commonly employed during the main Tet Offensive. Such boldness came at immense cost, however, for casualties in the border fights were both heavy and lopsided. At Dak To, for example, roughly 1,400 NVA soldiers were killed, compared with about 350 Americans and South Vietnamese.

The major event of Giap's preparatory phase was the siege of Khe Sanh, which began on January 21, 1968 and continued for 77 days. Khe Sanh was a small village in South Vietnam's northeast corner, and American Special Forces established an outpost nearby in 1962, the westernmost in a string of bases that ran along the southern edge of the demilitarized zone. By 1967, the Khe Sanh Combat Base (KSCB) was a key element in General Westmoreland's approach to the country's north, a bulwark protecting the northern provinces of Thua Thien and Quang Tri from Communist infiltration, as well as a base for Special Forces missions into Laos and reconnaissance flights over the Ho Chi Minh Trail. It housed a small airstrip, formidable defensive artillery, and a full battalion of Marines, with the Special Forces troops stationed a few miles west near the smaller village of Lang Vei.

Throughout 1967, the indications that Khe Sanh would be at the center of a major confrontation gradually piled up. The Marines and NVA fought a brief but savage battle there on the night of March 15, and between April 22 and May 11, there was a series of "hill fights," contests between the Third Marine Regiment and the NVA over control of the high ground in the area of Khe Sanh. While the Marines ultimately prevailed in these encounters, North Vietnamese resistance was stiff and unyielding. By September, two NVA battalions (about 1,600 men) had moved into the area, and by December, two full divisions (perhaps 20,000 men) were approaching Khe Sanh from the north.

With the example of France's catastrophic defeat in the 1954 siege of Dien Bien Phu prominent in his mind, General Westmoreland concluded that Khe Sanh would be the focus of the North Vietnamese war effort in 1968. Such an assault, perhaps the opening move in an attempt to overrun South Vietnam's northern provinces, would provide Westmoreland something he had long desired: an opportunity to bring his overwhelming firepower advantage to bear against massed NVA forces in a conventional pitched battle. Eager to take the fight to the North Vietnamese, and with "no intentions of sitting back to wait the enemy's move," early in January 1968, Westmoreland launched the first phase of Operation Niagara, aerial reconnaissance to identify and locate NVA and VC forces in the Khe Sanh area. (Westmoreland, 314).

Finally, on January 21, a force of about 300 NVA troops assaulted a Marine camp on Hill 861, just northeast of the Khe Sanh Combat Base. In brutal fighting, the Communists took the hill, then lost it again to a Marine counterattack. Shortly thereafter, NVA forces overran the village of Khe Sanh, forcing the Marines stationed there, along with numerous South Vietnamese civilians, to retreat to KSCB, which itself came under heavy artillery, mortar, and rocket fire. With perhaps 6,000 Marines surrounded by at least 20,000 and perhaps as many as 40,000 NVA troops, the siege of Khe Sanh had begun.

General Westmoreland responded with phase two of Operation Niagra: unprecedented aerial bombardment of NVA positions. By the time the siege was finally lifted in April, more than 25,000 missions had been flown over the Khe Sanh area, with more than 100,000 tons of bombs dropped.

Even now, the overall impact of these diversionary strikes is difficult to judge. In one sense, they were disastrous failures, "useless and bloody," in the words of North Vietnamese Colonel Tran Van Doc. (Davidson, 469) Ultimately, the Americans turned every assault back, often inflicting disproportionately heavy casualties in the process. Moreover, Giap had badly underestimated the Americans' strategic mobility; Westmoreland was able to deploy reinforcements to each new battle site and then quickly redeploy them back to the interior once the action had subsided. In that sense, the border strikes failed to draw American forces away from South Vietnam's urban centers as intended.

In another sense, however, the actions of Giap's preparatory phase helped to persuade the American leadership that the coming offensive would be focused on taking control of the northern provinces. In Washington, President Johnson took a personal, even obsessive, interest in the siege, devoting hours to studying a model of the military base he kept in the White House. "I don't want any damn Dinbinphoo," he scolded his military advisors. (Vandiver, 271). This obsessive American focus on Khe Sanh would make Giap's main offensive all the more shocking.

Marines of Company G, 2d Battalion, 3d Marines inch their way toward the summit of Hill 881N during the Hill fights. (USMC Photo A189161)

Close air support strikes of the 1st Marine Aircraft Wing and massive artillery fires paved the way for infantry assaults. (USMC Photo A421953)

Pictures taken during the siege

Chapter 4: The Main Offensive

When the main phase of the Tet Offensive finally came, Giap's meticulous, almost obsessive, focus on secrecy proved both a blessing and a curse for the North Vietnamese. On the one hand, various sources in the American and South Vietnamese defense establishments did predict a major Communist offensive in early 1968; the CIA's Saigon station actually distributed a report on this subject titled "The Big Gamble," and General Earle Wheeler, chairman of the Joint Chiefs of Staff, speculated on December 18 that the North might attempt a major thrust "similar to the desperate effort of the Germans in the Battle of the Bulge." (Arnold, 35) However, military officers completely misjudged its timing, focus, and scope. Throughout January, American forces captured Viet Cong plans for assaults on several southern cities, and even an audio tape announcing the "liberation" of Saigon and Hue, but Giap had been careful to compartmentalize his plans. None of the captured documents referenced a major, nationwide offensive, and while VC and NVA officers in the field may have vaguely understood that something big was coming, few knew anything concrete beyond their own specific orders. On the basis of these few, ambiguous indications, Westmoreland concluded, not unreasonably, that attacks on southern cities and towns would merely be limited feints intended to distract him from the main focus of the Communist offensive: Khe Sanh and the north. As one of Westmoreland's intelligence officers later recalled of American military attitudes prior to Tet, "Even had I known exactly what was to take place, it was so preposterous that I probably would have been unable to sell it to anybody." (Westmoreland, 421). That said, one American officer who deserves credit for seeing more clearly than his colleagues is Lieutenant General Frederick C. Weyand. Responsible for monitoring and protecting the region around Saigon, in December, Weyand noted unusual VC activity in the area and redeployed his troops closer to the capital. These reinforcements would be crucial in the defense of the city.

Weyand

Wheeler

On the other hand, however, the extreme compartmentalization that Giap imposed on his officers made close coordination of the Tet Offensive virtually impossible. This proved a major liability early on when the NVA and VC repeatedly failed to follow up on early successes by reinforcing, resupplying, and supporting units that had managed to take key positions. Instead, advance units were left to wither in the face of furious American and South Vietnamese counterattacks.

Even the timing of the offensive was badly mishandled. Giap had simply instructed his officers to open their assaults on "the first day of the Lunar New Year," meant to be the first day of Tet. However, North and South Vietnam at the time employed slightly different calendars, which placed the crucial day on January 30 and January 31 respectively. Further muddying the waters, late in January the North Vietnamese government proclaimed that the first day of Tet would be observed on January 29; the official explanation hinged on the intricacies of traditional

Vietnamese astrology, but the actual motivation was to allow North Vietnamese a chance to observe the holiday before the offensive began.

As a result, rather than breaking as a single massive wave in the early morning of January 31, as Giap had intended, the Tet Offensive opened with a trickle of attacks on the 30th. When these premature strikes, which took place at Nha Trang, Hoi An, Ban Me Thuot, Da Nang, Kontum, Pleiku, and Qui Nhon, were quickly repulsed, South Vietnamese President Thieu canceled the regular Tet ceasefire and General Westmoreland placed his troops on alert. Few in the American or South Vietnamese militaries yet understood the scope of the challenge they were facing, though Brigadier General Philip Davidson, the head of American military intelligence in South Vietnam, reportedly warned, "This is going to happen in the rest of the country tonight or tomorrow morning." (Dougan and Weiss, 12.).

President Thieu

Davidson

Davidson, of course, proved correct. Early in the morning of January 31, at least 80,000 combined NVA and VC troops struck cities, towns, and military installations throughout South Vietnam, and for the most part, despite the last-minute warnings, they achieved complete or partial surprise. Altogether, the Communists assaulted virtually all of South Vietnam's cities, 3/4ths of its provincial capitals, 64 district capitals, dozens of towns, and every significant American airfield. Major targets ranged from Hue, Tam Ky, and Quang Tri in the north, through Tuy Hoa and Phan Thiet in the center, to Saigon in the south, and Ben Tre, Go Cong, Kien Tuong, Dinh Tuong, Can Tho, My Tho, and Vinh Long in the Mekong Delta region. In addition, the American military bases at Phu Bai, Chu Lai, Bong Song, An Khe, and Long Bien (as well as the SVA headquarters at Long Bien) came under sustained attack.

A picture of American soldiers fighting at Battle of Hamo Village

These strikes were determined, carefully planned, and often, in their early stages, highly successful. Typically, they opened with a blistering artillery or rocket barrage. Next came small units of combat engineers, who sought out and exploited weak points in the defenses of a city, town, or outpost, opening holes through which the main force Communist troops could enter. The officers leading these assaults generally had excellent intelligence on the layout of their targets, and in a few cases they had even personally reconnoitered them (incognito) in the months before Tet. They also, as often as not, had confederates already infiltrated into the cities or towns they targeted. Where they managed—however briefly—to seize control, Communist forces quickly identified and executed "collaborators" with the Thieu government, including officials, teachers, SVA officers, priests, business owners, and landlords. They also immediately set their propaganda teams to work attempting to rouse civilians against the South Vietnamese government and its American patrons. Leveraging the support of the Southern public, of course, was essential to the long-term success of Giap's program.

In the country's north (the I Corps Tactical Zone, in the American military parlance of the time), the offensive was largely carried out by NVA regulars. In addition to the ongoing siege of the Marine base at Khe Sanh, NVA troops launched a powerful assault on Quang Tri and actually managed to capture the ancient capital of Hue. Along the northern coast, only fierce resistance from local South Vietnamese Army units saved the city of Da Nang—South Vietnam's second largest—after an NVA assault achieved near total surprise. Indeed, one of the bitterest lessons of Tet for Giap and his staff was the grit and determination exhibited by the oft-maligned SVA. One of the guiding assumptions of the Tet planners was that Southern soldiers suffered from lax discipline and low morale, that they resented their American allies, felt no loyalty to the Saigon government, and would simply crumble and desert in the face of a sustained assault. In fact, South Vietnamese Army units largely remained intact, and in Da Nang and elsewhere they proved themselves very much capable of standing against the NVA in a pitched battle.

Further south, in the II Corps Tactical Zone, both NVA and VC attacks were widespread, including even a rocket assault on the American naval base at Cam Ranh Bay. As in the north, SVA units played a crucial role in the allied counterattack in the II Corps area. In Nha Trang a combination of U.S. Special Forces and SVA Rangers fought back a concerted attack on the city and nearby Naval Training Center. At Ban Me Thout and Qui Nhon, local SVA units overcame VC and NVA assaults without American support. In fact, in Ban Me Thout, an active intelligence network and quick-thinking on the part of the local commander effectively nullified the VC's surprise advantage, and in Dalat, two SVA security companies, reinforced by cadets from the local Vietnamese National Military Academy, managed to hold out against two VC battalions.

Further to the south, in the Mekong Delta region (the IV Corps Tactical Zone), the character of the fighting was different. Here, the SVA units were less effective, due in no small measure to the fact that the South Vietnamese general in charge more or less abrogated his responsibilities, leaving the initiative to the Americans. Further, few NVA units made it this far south, so the offensive in this zone was largely carried out by local Viet Cong. Perhaps for this reason, the conflict in the delta was particularly brutal and hard-fought. In My Tho, for example, two American battalions sought to relieve an SVA division threatened by four Viet Cong battalions, and the result was bloody urban warfare. In this case, the Americans were from a combined Army-Navy unit, the Mobile Riverine Force (MRF). Designed to operate in small armored ships cruising the maze of paddies and canals that made up the Mekong Delta, MRF battalions were neither armed nor trained for close-quarters urban warfare, but nevertheless, over the course of three days, the Americans advanced house-by-house and street-by-street to finally secure the urban core from the VC

When Ben Tre, a river city near the coast, was partially occupied by a force of perhaps 2,500 determined VC troops, the Americans and South Vietnamese responded with a massive air and artillery barrage. Such extreme measures ultimately killed or drove off the VC occupiers, but at the cost of leveling entire neighborhoods of Ben Tre. In the aftermath of the battle, the journalist Peter Arnett famously reported that an anonymous American major had told him, "It became necessary to destroy the town to save it." (Braestrup, 1:254). Historians investigating the battle have since called this account into question, and a retired officer who claims to have been Arnett's "major" has accused the reporter of misquoting him. Whatever the truth of the matter, however, the quote, and the notion that America was engaged in a hopeless project of destroying South Vietnam in order to save it, resonated powerfully with a bitter and disillusioned American public. It was reported as fact in multiple newspapers, magazines, and television news programs and became a touchstone of the burgeoning domestic antiwar movement.

Arnett

Taken as a whole, the strikes that made up the main Tet Offensive shocked the American and South Vietnamese military establishments with both their reach and their ferocity. They commanded attention from news establishments around the globe, and in America, the offensive helped to spark a very public reassessment of the country's commitment to fighting Communism in Indochina. In all of these respects, the offensive represented a success for Giap and a major turning point in the war.

In a narrower, more tactical sense, however, the initial phases of the offensive were failures. Coordination from unit to unit was poor, and while many NVA and VC forces managed to capture key strategic points, they had little success in defending these gains against rapid and blistering allied counterattacks. In most cities, the Americans and South Vietnamese managed to re-establish control in just a few days, and by the first week after Tet, the Communist offensive had largely run its course. Thus, despite the surprise, American military officers could be forgiven for claiming Tet as a victory, and as North Vietnamese General Tran Van Tra later assessed the offensive, "We did not correctly evaluate the specific balance of forces between ourselves and the enemy, did not fully realize that the enemy still had considerable capabilities and that our capabilities were limited, and set requirements that were beyond our actual strength. . . . We suffered large sacrifices and losses with regard to manpower and material, especially cadres at the various echelons, which clearly weakened us. Afterwards, we were not only unable to retain the gains we had made but had to overcome a myriad of difficulties in 1969 and 1970 so that the revolutionary could stand firm in the storm." (Tran, 35)

There is much truth in this assessment, but even so, in a few important locations like Saigon, Hue, and Khe Sanh, the fighting was so dramatic, fierce, and protracted that it came to dominate popular interpretations and memories of the Tet Offensive as a whole.

Chapter 5: Saigon

A picture of fighting in and around Saigon

Perhaps more than any other, the Communist assault on Saigon came to symbolize the brittle, hollow nature of America's position in Vietnam. Saigon was South Vietnam's capital, the site of the Presidential Palace, the American Embassy, and massive American air base, and the headquarters of both the South Vietnamese Army and the American MACV. There were more than 100 American military outposts, bases, and installations in the area around Saigon, but in a nod to Vietnamese national sentiment, defense of the city proper was largely the province of the SVA and national police force.

Before the Tet Offensive, the city was widely considered a safe haven. Originally a city of about 1 million, Saigon's population had tripled thanks to the flow of refugees fleeing violence and Viet Cong insurgents in the countryside. Prior to 1968, Saigon had rarely been touched, and never seriously threatened, by the war. In the wake of Tet, however, residents were left to wonder if anywhere in South Vietnam was beyond the reach of the Viet Cong.

The assault on Saigon ultimately included no fewer than 35 NVA and Viet Cong battalions approaching the capital from all sides. Some, indeed, had already secretly infiltrated Saigon before Tet began. Early in the morning of January 31, a force of more than 4,000 under the command of NVA General Tran Do struck, and in some cases they briefly overran strategic targets in the city's urban core. Around 1:30 a.m., for example, Independence Palace, on Nguyen Du Street in the city's east, came under attack by a force of Viet Cong sappers disguised in SVA uniforms. The group managed to breach the palace gate with B-40 rockets before they were met with determined resistance from the local security force. Pushed back, the Viet Cong sappers took refuge in an apartment building, which they defended tenaciously. It took two full days for the SVA and American forces to clear them out.

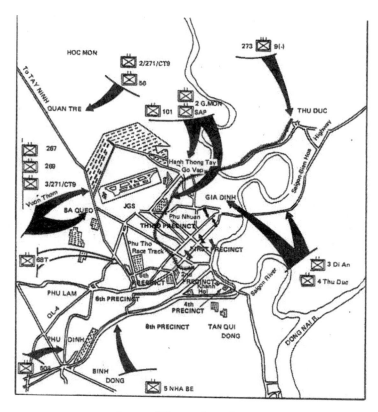

A map of the attacks on Saigon

A picture of South Vietnamese soldiers defending Saigon

The offensive followed a similar pattern elsewhere in Saigon. A blistering assault on the Vietnamese Navy headquarters, to the capital's south, was rapidly turned back, but in the north, Viet Cong forces succeeded in taking the headquarters of Armored Command and Artillery Command, only to find that the tanks and artillery pieces ordinarily stored there had been disabled or removed. In the city's east, a small group of Viet Cong guerrillas, some disguised as SVA soldiers, took the headquarters of South Vietnam's government radio station. This might have been an important propaganda victory, as broadcasts from the Saigon station reached across South Vietnam and the team had brought audio tapes declaring the fall of Saigon and immanent nationwide Communist uprising, but a quick-thinking South Vietnamese technician alerted the station's transmitting tower, which cut off its connection before the tapes could be broadcast. The Viet Cong guerrillas barricaded the entrances and managed to hold out for about six hours. Expected reinforcements failed to materialize, however, and they were eventually overwhelmed by a company of SVA paratroopers. As this suggests, while VC teams often succeeded in capturing their initial objectives, they lacked the coordination, supplies, and reinforcements necessary to capitalize on these early successes. Isolated, and with little or no guidance from above, few of the Viet Cong teams in Saigon managed to survive long in the face of the inevitable allied counterassault.

In addition to highly visible targets such as Independence Palace or the national radio broadcaster, Viet Cong teams also struck local police stations, SVA barracks, and even the homes of military officers and bureaucrats. In the neighborhoods they overran, VC guerrillas went house to house for individuals on their lists of collaborators and traitors, and when identified, these traitors were presented before "people's courts" and summarily executed. In the words of one witness, "They guarded the street, checked houses and ID cards, and forbade us to leave. Soldiers on leave were arrested and shot on the spot. Ordinary people weren't arrested, but weren't allowed to leave the area." (Dougan and Weiss, 19).

Of course, summary executions were by no means restricted to the Viet Cong; in the chaos, violence, and desperation of Tet, neither side was inclined to take prisoners. In one famous incident, General Nguyen Ngoc Loan, the head of South Vietnam's national police force, personally executed an unarmed Viet Cong guerrilla standing bound and in full view of a group of journalists. The photograph of Loan with his revolver to the guerrilla's head became an instant sensation and was splashed across newspapers around the world, a symbol, to many, of the senseless brutality of the war. "They killed many Americans and many of my men," Loan explained to the reporters. "Buddha will understand. Do you?" (Oberdorfer, 161 – 71).

Loan

Without a doubt, the most heavily symbolic target to be struck that day was the American Embassy. Operationally, the brief assault on the embassy was an abject failure, but as propaganda, however, the news that the Viet Cong had somehow struck at the nerve-center of the American presence in South Vietnam was a major coup. The embassy compound, a four-acre plot off Thong Nhat Boulevard, was carefully sealed off from the rest of Saigon, heavily guarded and surrounded by a wall 8 feet high. At the heart of the compound was the embassy itself, a sturdy, imposing six-story building completed in September 1967 at a cost of more than $2.5 million. More than any other location in the capital, to supporters and opponents alike, the embassy represented the beating heart of American power in Vietnam.

Pictures of the Embassy in 1968

The assault on the embassy was brief but dramatic. Around 2:45 a.m., a team of Viet Cong sappers detonated a charge on the compound's perimeter, breaching the outer wall. A platoon of Viet Cong rushed into the gap, but they met immediate heavy resistance from local military police (MPs), who killed the platoon leader and left the remainder of the VC force without direction. Rudderless, the Viet Cong fortified their position in the outer compound as best they could and managed to hold out for about six hours against the American guards and MPs who flooded the compound. The VC commandos never reached the embassy building itself, but its outer face was riddled with bullets and the Great Seal of the United States was knocked from the front door. Eventually, reinforcements in the form of the 101st Airborne Division arrived by helicopter and managed to clear the remnants of Viet Cong from the compound.

American news reporters, photographers, and cameramen, many of whom were staying at downtown hotels just a few blocks away, reached the embassy compound before the fighting had ended. In the darkness and confusion, several reported erroneously that the chancery building— and even the embassy building itself—had been occupied. Combined with shocking images of American MPs dead and wounded on the embassy grounds, these reports appeared on the front pages of newspapers across the United States on the morning of February 1. General Westmoreland, who arrived at the embassy shortly after the compound had been secured, sought desperately to correct the record, giving reporters tours through the compound and insisting that "the enemy's well-laid plans went afoul." (Oberdorfer, 34). Technically, Westmoreland was correct, since the chancery and embassy buildings had never been breached and the attack itself had quickly fizzled out. Nonetheless, in the midst of a wave of devastating surprise attacks across South Vietnam, and with VC guerrillas only recently driven from the embassy compound, his confidence rang false to the increasingly suspicious press corps. In the words of a reporter for the *Washington Post*, "The reporters could hardly believe their ears. Westmoreland was standing in the ruins and saying everything was great." (Arnold, 57).

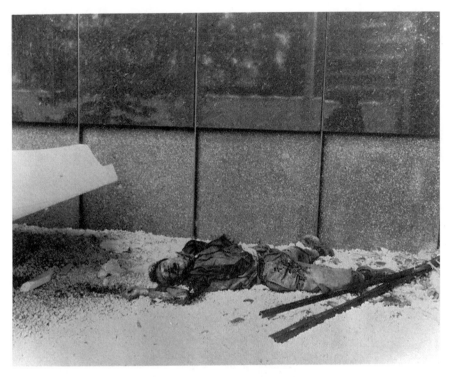

Pictures of Viet Cong sappers dead outside the embassy

Whether fairly or not, many observers interpreted the Tet Offensive, and particularly the embassy strike, as evidence that Westmoreland's frequent claims of progress had been insincere. Walter Cronkite reportedly responded to news of the embassy attack with furious incredulity: "What the hell is going on? I thought we were winning this war!" (Wyatt, 168).

Chapter 6: Hue

Pictures of Marines fighting at Hue

While the assault on Saigon drew the most international attention, the bitter conflict over control of the city of Hue was perhaps the most protracted and hardest-fought battle of the Tet Offensive. In the words of Don Oberdorfer, who covered the battle for the *Washington Post*, "The twenty-five day struggle for Hue was the longest and bloodiest ground action of the Tet offensive and, quite possibly, the longest and bloodiest single action of the Second Indochina War." (Summers, 134).

Between 1802 and 1945, Hue had been the seat of Vietnam's Nguyen emperors, and the ancient capital remained a cultural, intellectual, and religious center, easily the most venerated city in Vietnam. The Old City (or "Citadel") north of the Song River, in particular, was a maze of ancient temples, luxuriant gardens, grand palaces, and narrow stone alleyways, which made the city a tourist's dream, as many a rueful GI would later note, but also "a rifle-toting infantryman's nightmare." (Murphy, 189).

Loathe to be held responsible for the destruction of the ancient capital, the Viet Cong had mostly steered clear of Hue, and with the exception of an occasional mortar attack, the city had mostly been secure and free of violence. With the planned general uprising of the Tet Offensive, however, Hue's cultural status could no longer protect the city from its own strategic position.

By 1968, Hue was a city of nearly 150,000, making it South Vietnam's third-largest after Saigon and Da Nang. It was the capital of Thua Thien Province, a linchpin for control of the country's northeast, and thanks to its position on Highway 1, just 60 miles south of the Demilitarized Zone, a key point for provisioning allied troops along the northern border.

The Communist assault on Hue was carefully planned. As many as 8,000 VC and NVA troops, specially trained in streetfighting techniques, took part in the initial offensive, designed to overwhelm the local garrison, cut the city off from allied reinforcements, and inspire the populace to rise up against Saigon. The troops were armed with detailed maps of the city, along with lists of "cruel tyrants and reactionary elements"—government officials, landlords, military officers, and other anti-Communist figures—to be apprehended.

As the battle for Hue expanded in scope and significance, the original 10 Communist battalions in and around the city eventually doubled to a peak of 20, and at the outset, the allied defense of Hue was desperate and piecemeal. The only American troops in the city when the assault commenced were the 200 men of the MACV advisory compound, stationed in the "New City" on the south bank of the Song River. The Phu Bai Combat Base, home to Task Force X-Ray, of the 1st Marine Division, was located 8 miles south of the city, too far off to respond effectively to the first surprise attack. Moreover, most of the task force, commanded by Brigadier General Foster C. "Frosty" LaHue, had only just been transferred to the area from Da Nang and were not yet familiar with the terrain.

LaHue

In their absence, the brunt of the initial assault fell upon the 1st Infantry Division of the South Vietnamese Army, headquartered in the Citadel's northwest. The division was formidable, and its commander, Brigadier General Ngo Quang Truong, was among the most capable in the SVA. Nonetheless, at the time of the assault, Truong was severely short-staffed; the majority of his men were on leave for the Tet holiday, and of those that remained, most were stationed outside the city. Few imagined that the Communists would break with precedent and attack Hue proper, so the only sizeable SVA contingent actually inside the city on January 31 was the Hac Bao reconnaissance company, the so-called "Black Panthers," stationed at the Citadel's airstrip.

Truong

The operation commenced at 3:40 a.m. on January 31 with a rocket and mortar assault from the west. Following the barrage, three Communist battalions (two NVA and one VC) entered Hue from the southwest and linked up with groups of infiltrators who, in the guise of Tet pilgrims, had been stockpiling weapons and supplies inside the city for weeks. Once inside, the troops fanned out, crossed the Song River, and established control over most of the Citadel.

In the north, Brigadier General Truong and his men managed to hold out at the 1st Infantry Division's headquarters, as did the Hac Bao company at the airfield. In the south, the Americans in the MACV advisory compound withstood two NVA assaults and a mortar barrage, but they were in no position to launch a counter-attack. Short on both men and supplies, they fortified their position as best they could and sent out a desperate request for reinforcements.

With the exception of these few pockets of resistance, the entire city was in Communist hands by the middle of the morning. VC cadres wasted little time in establishing revolutionary committees and unleashing a reign of terror on the civilian populace. Evidence uncovered from mass graves suggests that at least 3,000 "cruel tyrants and reactionary elements" were arrested and executed before the allies re-took the city.

Pictures of victims of the Hue Massacre being reinterred

In the first chaotic days of Tet, American officers, including both Generals LaHue at Phu Bai and Westmoreland in Saigon, drastically underestimated the scale of the Communist forces assembled at Hue. As a result, the early American response was grossly insufficient. On January 31, General LaHue sent a single Marine company north up Highway 1, but the rescue force was turned back at the outskirts of the city by stiff NVA resistance. Reinforced by a second relief force, the Marines managed to reach the beleaguered MACV compound by late afternoon. Ordered north across the Nguyen Hoang Bridge into the Old City, the Marines encountered a mass of fire from NVA units in fortified positions along the north bank of the Song River. After two hours of hard fighting, and with fully one-third of their numbers killed or wounded, the Marines finally withdrew back to the New City.

Finally recognizing the true nature of the challenge they faced in Hue, Westmoreland and his staff began sending in significant reinforcements, both Marines from the 1st Division and (along the outskirts of the city) troops from the Army's 1st Cavalry Division. They also placed the aggressive and capable Colonel Stanley S. Hughes in command of all American forces in Hue.

Under Hughes, the Marines began moving south and west from the MACV compound, rooting the NVA out block-by-block and driving them into the Cavalry units surrounding the city. For the Marines, who had not been trained in urban warfare, re-taking the New City required mastering unfamiliar new tactics in the midst of combat. Even worse, at such close quarters, the Americans' usual advantages of air superiority and overwhelming firepower meant little. It took just over two weeks of bitter combat for the Marines to re-establish control over the New City and another two weeks to mop up remaining pockets of resistance.

Hughes

Meanwhile, the allied counterattack in the Old City north of the Song River fell to the SVA forces under General Truong. This decision made reasonable operational sense, since both the Black Panthers and General Truong's headquarters were already in the north. Even so, there was a public-relations dimension as well; American actions in the ancient capital were bound to arouse national sensitivities, particularly among conservative Buddhists. In the words of LaHue's superior Lieutenant General Robert Cushman, "I wasn't about to open up on the old palace and all the historical buildings there." (Shulimson et al, 176).

Despite reinforcements, however, Truong found his forces unable to make progress in re-taking the Citadel, particularly the fortress-like imperial palace, and after more than a week of failed attempts, he requested assistance from Hughes' Marines. Combat north of the river proved even more bitter and protracted than the fighting in the New City had been. On February 10, with SVA units concentrated on the southwest corner, Marines launched a concerted assault on the

Citadel's eastern edge. By this point, Communist positions were extremely well-fortified, and, despite being badly outnumbered, the NVA defenders were unrelenting, forcing the Americans to pay for every inch of territory they gained. By February 22, the Americans had opened a hole in the eastern wall of the palace, and on the night of February 23, a massive SVA assault from the west finally overcame the last of the NVA and VC defenders inside.

By March 2, with more than 200 Americans, more than 350 South Vietnamese, and perhaps as many as 8,000 Communists dead, the battle for Hue was finally over. The operation had been costly for the allies, and even more so for the Communists, but the true losers were Hue's civilian population. By the time the battle ended, more than 100,000 were homeless, and more than 5,000 had died or disappeared in the fighting. In the words of one observer, the war had left Hue "a shattered, stinking hulk, its streets choked with rubble and rotting bodies." (Moss, 279)

Chapter 7: Khe Sanh

Though it is not technically recognized as such, it could be argued the Tet Offensive had begun on January 21 with the NVA assault on the Khe Sanh Combat Base (KSCB). In that sense, it is appropriate that this was also where the offensive would finally come to an end. In fact, throughout Tet, both General Westmoreland and President Johnson remained focused on the plight of the Marines at Khe Sanh, convinced that the attacks on Saigon, Da Nang, Hue, and elsewhere were merely distractions from the main event.

The base was in such a remote location that one Marin complained, "When you're at Khe Sanh, you're not really anywhere." (Willbanks, 58). Given that fact, the administration's preoccupation may be surprising, but Westmoreland hoped to use Khe Sanh as a base for a future assault on Communist positions in eastern Laos. He was also tantalized by the possibility that the siege of Khe Sanh might expose the usually cautious NVA to American airpower. As one Marine put it, "The Marines at Khe Sanh were bait; chum liberally spread around the Khe Sanh tactical area to entice large military forces of North Vietnam from the depths of their sanctuaries to the exposed shallows of America's high-technology killing machine." (Gilbert and Head, 196).

For his part, President Johnson feared the consequences of a major loss such as the French had suffered at Dien Bien Phu. Indeed, by insisting so loudly and publicly on the importance of Khe Sanh, the American leadership had effectively painted itself into a corner. In the words of General Maxwell Taylor, "It was apparent that the die was cast and we would have to fight it out on this line. . . We ourselves had done a great deal to build up the importance of Khe Sanh in the minds of the public, and it was going to be difficult to explain to our people or anyone else that Khe Sanh was a minor outpost and the outcome of the battle unimportant." (Dougan and Weiss, 45).

Fortunately, the position of the 6,000 Marines at Khe Sanh was never as desperate as that of the French at Dien Bien Phu. Though they were surrounded by 20,000 or more NVA troops, the

Americans maintained control of the region's air space, as well as a small airstrip, a vital lifeline that could be used for resupply and, if necessary, reinforcements. Altogether, American aircraft delivered about 160 tons of supplies to the base every day, and air crews flew regular offensive sorties over the Khe Sanh area, up to 300 daily at their peak. The most punishing of these sorties were carried out by long-distance B-52 bombers based in Okinawa, Guam, and Thailand. Over the course of the siege, B-52s dropped no less than 50,000 tons of explosives on NVA positions. Moreover, the Marines retained control over the strategic high points around Khe Sanh, which allowed them to send patrols out into the surrounding countryside and successfully keep their NVA besiegers off-balance.

Even so, the Marines at Khe Sanh suffered through regular rocket, mortar, and artillery attacks on all sides, and NVA forces successfully overran the nearby Special Forces base at Lang Vei. On February 29, after the Tet Offensive had died down nearly everywhere else, the NVA launched a major frontal assault on the base's southeastern corner. Wave upon wave of attackers fell upon the SVA rangers stationed there but fell back in the face of massive firepower and the Americans' air support. After this point, unknown to the American leadership, NVA forces began gradually to withdraw from the Khe Sanh area. On April 8, the American 1st Cavalry Division finally managed to push westward along Route 9 to Khe Sanh, lifting the long siege.

Without question, the operation had been a disaster for the Communists. Altogether, the combined Marine and SVA forces at Khe Sanh lost no more than 233 men killed and 1,014 wounded. On the NVA side, however, perhaps as many as 15,000 were killed in the failed attempt to take the base. Reportedly, some NVA units suffered 90% casualties, largely due to the relentless B-52 bombing raids. In this respect, at least, General Westmoreland got his wish: the siege at Khe Sanh had drawn considerable NVA forces into the open, where America's overwhelming firepower had proven decisive. As the general exalted, "Without question, the amount of firepower put on that piece of real estate exceeded anything that had ever been seen before in history by any foe, and the enemy was hurt, his back was broken, by airpower." (Dougan and Weiss, 51).

It was a tactical victory, but the real issue was whether the American public would conclude that such a victory was worth the cost.

Chapter 8: The Aftermath of the Tet Offensive

By the time the siege of Khe Sanh was lifted in April, the initial Tet Offensive had been repulsed throughout South Vietnam. Indeed, in many American accounts, the end of fighting at Khe Sanh is identified as the final action of the Tet Offensive. To the North Vietnamese, however, the "general offensive, general uprising" of Tet was a longer-term project that would continue at least through September. In the words of Tran Van Tra, while the initial offensive had failed to spark a widespread popular uprising or significantly weaken allied military capacity, it had nonetheless "sent shudders throughout the enemy's vital points, and destabilized its military, political, and economic foundations throughout South Vietnam," creating an opportunity for North Vietnam to "continue strong assaults and compensate for . . . earlier shortcomings in order to win even bigger victories." (Werner and Huynh, 48).

Nonetheless, the troops who carried out the initial offensive had suffered heavy casualties. This was particularly true of the local Viet Cong guerrillas, who had made up the bulk of the Communist forces in the south. These networks of disciplined and highly-motivated guerrilla cadres had survived for years in the face of the American and South Vietnamese militaries by keeping to the shadows and avoiding large-scale pitched battles. In that sense, the initial Tet attacks granted General Westmoreland and his officers exactly what they had long wished for: traditional pitched battles against the VC. The result had been as bloody as it was predictable, with an overwhelmingly lopsided body count and the decimation of Viet Cong networks throughout South Vietnam. A continued offensive would require massive reinforcements. Thus, through March and April, perhaps as many as 90,000 NVA reinforcements were sent down the Ho Chi Minh Trail to infiltrate the South.

May saw a punishing new wave of strikes across South Vietnam, known as the so-called "Mini-Tet" attacks. NVA troops struck Saigon on May 5, and heavy fighting raged there, off and on, through early June. Even after that, rocket and artillery barrages regularly targeted the capital for weeks. Casualties throughout "Mini-Tet" were heavy, and though it's often forgotten, American casualties were higher in May 1968 than in any other month of the war. Hundreds of civilians were killed in Saigon alone, and tens of thousands (perhaps as many as 200,000 across the country) were displaced from their homes.

In August, the NVA's focus moved on to South Vietnamese Army fortifications in the Mekong Delta region, as well as American bases northwest of the capital. As with the initial Tet attacks, the operations between May and August 1968 proved damaging to the Communist forces, who suffered massive casualties before falling back in the face of allied firepower. Furthermore, without the advantage of surprise, few NVA strikes achieved the dramatic early victories they had enjoyed in January and February.

Nonetheless, from the perspective of American policymakers, the "Mini-Tet" attacks made a bad situation even worse. They kept Vietnam in the headlines and helped to convince a growing number of Americans that the war was fundamentally unwinnable. During the earliest days of the Tet Offensive, Americans naturally responded to the Communist offensive with a wave of patriotism and belligerence, and in early February, a national poll reported that fully 55% of Americans supported increasing America's military commitment to defeating Communism in South Vietnam. However, the steady drip of violent stories and images that came out during the first half of 1968 effectively soured that initial burst of confidence and defiance, further eroding Americans' already shaky confidence in their leaders and the war they had chosen to fight.

There is no more significant instance of this sea change in public opinion than the very public agony of CBS newsman Walter Cronkite. Cronkite's conversion from supporter to outspoken war skeptic—simultaneously a cause, an effect, and a microcosm of the larger national reassessment—did not come easily. While his doubts about the war effort had multiplied in the years preceding Tet, he had been hesitant to abandon his public stance as an objective journalist:

> "I had resisted doing commentary on the *Evening News* even when it had been suggested to me. I was concerned about whether it's possible as a professional journalist to wear two hats. But when Tet came along, the public was already divided and confused. We had been told that the war was practically over, that there was light at the end of the tunnel, that we had won the hearts and minds, that the Viet Cong was decreasing in strength and popular support, and then suddenly it can conduct a military operation of the scale and the intensity that it did in Tet. Well, everybody was throwing up their hands saying "God, what in the world is happening out there?" And we decided that we had pretty good credibility of having been as impartial as it's possible to be, and maybe it's time to go out there and just do some pieces on what it looks like and try to give some guidance.

> "My personal approach had been impartial because I found it hard to make up my own mind. In the early stages I thought we should be involved in trying to preserve a territory where democracy might be permitted to flourish in Southeast Asia. I began to get opposed when the military commitment was made. I didn't think we ought to have our troops there. And then I got more and more concerned as more and more troops [went out]. My particular concern was that the Administration did not tell us the truth about the nature or size of the commitment that was going to be required. And I think that's where the Administration lost the support of the American people—in trying to pretend it was something we could do with our left hand, without asking the people at home to share the heavy responsibility. At any rate, I went out there and what I saw led me to the conclusions that I made." (Willenson, 195 – 96).

In the middle February, Cronkite traveled to South Vietnam, investigating the state of the conflict and even interviewing marines in Hue while the battle there still raged. Returning to the United States in late February, Cronkite pulled no punches. Describing South Vietnam as a "burned and blasted and weary land," Cronkite announced, "We have been too often disappointed by the optimism of the American leaders. . . . To say that we are closer to victory today is to believe, in the face of evidence, the optimists who have been wrong in the past. . . . To say that we are mired in stalemate seems the only realistic, yet unsatisfactory conclusion. . . . It seems now more certain than ever that the bloody experience of Vietnam is to end in a stalemate. . . . It is increasingly clear to this reporter that the only rational way out then will be to negotiate, not as victors, but as honorable people who lived up to their pledge to defend democracy, and did the best they could." (Karnow, 547)

President Johnson allegedly responded to Cronkite's report with the comment, "If I've lost Cronkite, I've lost middle America." Reflecting on events much later, Cronkite himself was surprised by the impact of his commentary, and particularly its effect on the president: "I didn't expect it to be that effective It should have shocked the President only if he didn't know the full scale of the thing himself. I think he may have been as surprised by Tet as everybody else was, and while the military was putting up a brave front—'Oh, boy, we sucked them right into our trap and we've given them a great, magnificent military blow from which they'll never recover"—it was an optimism that, my God, you couldn't see on the ground out there. The Viet Cong was right in the city of Saigon. That was what kind of turned so many of us at that point into saying, "Come on, now. This is the end. Stop it.'" (Willenson, 196).

Cronkite in Vietnam

Indeed, despite some claims to the contrary, the ferocity and scope of the Tet Offensive appeared to have come as a massive shock to both the military command and the Johnson administration. Diplomat Richard Holbrooke, a member of the Johnson White House's Vietnam group who had earlier been an assistant to US Ambassador Henry Cabot Lodge, Jr. in Saigon, recalled, "There was an enormous confusion in the period from January 30, 1968, to March 30, 1968. Notwithstanding all the memoirs that have been written claiming that intelligence predicted the Tet offensive, the simple fact is that the Tet offensive caught the Administration unprepared. That's a fact. You can always go back later and find the intelligence that predicted [an attack], but we weren't ready for it in Washington. I was in [Undersecretary of State Nicholas] Katzenbach's office then, and I can tell you that there was horror and pandemonium all the way to the top. [Secretary of State Dean] Rusk and Katzenbach sent me out to Vietnam ten days later to make a personal assessment. I saw [Lodge's successor, US Ambassador Ellsworth] Bunker and [MACV commander General William] Westmoreland, and [Joint United States Public Affairs Office head] Barry Zorthian and [Deputy Assistant Secretary of State for East Asian and Pacific Affairs] Phil Habib and the others and with the exception of Habib, they were all in a state of shock, too." (Willenson, 149 – 50).

Under the circumstances, then, it is hardly surprising that American press coverage of the Tet Offensive and its fallout grew increasingly cynical, mistrustful of authority, and pessimistic. Even among historians and observers who believe that the prevailing narrative of the Tet Offensive has been badly misguided, and that it was actually a strategic victory for the Americans and South Vietnamese, it is generally acknowledged that the press response was at the very least an understandable reaction to the excessive optimism of the administration before the campaign. Peter Braestrup, for example, was a Marine in the Korean War, and later a combat correspondent in Vietnam for *New York Times*, and in a retrospective interview, he asserted that while he personally viewed Tet as a defeat for the North Vietnamese, the bleak tone of American press coverage was essentially due to the Johnson administration's ineptitude: "The fact that Tet was a setback for the other side, you can't blame the press for not knowing right then. Nobody knew it then. But since there was no leadership, they magnified the damage and prolonged the image of a great disaster…We wanted to call the score, so we did. We were reflecting the political reality back here, and confusing it with the military reality. Tet came after a great propaganda campaign. Johnson was hoist by his own petard and newsmen love that. Johnson had set himself up. He was trying to buy time and buy support for the war. And for the first time in American history, a field commander, Westmoreland, had allowed himself to be snookered into becoming a political spokesman. It was his vanity. He loved being on TV and he came home twice at Johnson's behest to speak, and it tainted him not only in the eyes of the press but in the eyes of a lot of military men. Westmoreland had in effect taken the king's shilling and become a propagandist—a soldier for the administration." (Willenson, 109).

In such a poisonous, confused atmosphere, official claims of an American victory in the Tet Offensive, whatever their merits, were bound to ring hollow. As Vermont Senator George Aiken declared, "If this is a failure, I hope the Viet Cong never have a major success." (Olson and Roberts, 186). In this sense, then, Giap's offensive was a genuine success; it may not have precipitated a general uprising in South Vietnam as intended, but it had dramatically changed the tone of public debate in the United States.

Perhaps the most significant casualty of the Tet Offensive was the presidency of Lyndon Baines Johnson. Following the assassination of John F. Kennedy, President Johnson had won an overwhelming re-election, with the highest percentage of the popular vote of any presidential election in modern American history, in November 1964. Over the next few years, however, Johnson's popularity and public image were gradually dragged down by a slowing economy and the worsening course of the Vietnam War, a war that Johnson had always viewed in private with a combination of apprehension and disdain. Even so, as late as November 1967, with General Westmoreland loudly insisting that victory was just around the corner, public approval of Johnson's war leadership remained positive at 51%.

However, by late February, with news of the Tet Offensive and the siege of Khe Sanh saturating the headlines, that number had plummeted to 32%, and by late March, it had fallen even further to just 26%. On March 10, popular anxiety was magnified when a *New York Times* article reported that in the wake of Tet, General Westmoreland had requested more than 200,000 reinforcements. This was somewhat misleading; Westmoreland had desired additional troops long before Tet, but not as a defensive measure. Instead, he had advocated taking the war to the enemy with massive offensives in both North Vietnam and Eastern Laos. With the Johnson administration unwilling to commit to the national mobilization that such an operation would necessitate, Westmoreland's proposal was a nonstarter. In February 1968, however, Joint Chiefs of Staff Chairman General Earle Wheeler apparently concluded that he could use the drama of Tet as a pretext to pressure Johnson to approve a large-scale mobilization that would include calling up the national reserves.

Wheeler appears to have desired this mobilization not so much to escalate the war in Vietnam as to shore up the American military's larger strategic position worldwide. Nonetheless, he urged Westmoreland to request reinforcements both to replace the men lost during the Tet Offensive and to respond to the NVA's improved position in South Vietnam. Westmoreland's official request for about 100,000 troops to be deployed in May and another 100,000 to be held for possible future deployment, was met with disbelief in Washington. In particular, the general's contention that the NVA had increased its troop numbers in the south did not square with his earlier claims that those same forces had been decimated. Wheeler had also made the jarring assertion that Tet "was a very near thing. . . . We suffered a loss, there can be no doubt about it." In the words of historian Richard Falk, Westmoreland's request "significantly hardened the impression among the hesitant in Washington and the media that Tet was an enormous, unacknowledged American defeat, and that the war, if seriously resumed, would be an even greater drain than it already was, and this the United States could not long afford either politically or economically." (Falk, 19).

Some in the Johnson administration even concluded, with some justification, that the military was attempting to railroad the civilian government into expanding the war. When news of Westmoreland's request for reinforcements was published, it was widely interpreted as an admission that America was losing the war.

Unsurprisingly then, with Johnson's popularity in apparent free fall, critics of the president— both opportunistic and sincere—grew more vocal. Senate Majority Leader Mike Mansfield of Montana, for example, had long been a Johnson ally in domestic matters, most notably as a crucial supporter of the Great Society programs and 1964 Civil Rights Act. He had publicly opposed American involvement in Vietnam since 1962, however, and in the wake of Tet, he underlined that opposition: "From the outset, it was not an American responsibility, and it is not now an American responsibility, to win a victory for any particular Vietnamese group, or to defeat any particular Vietnamese group." Furthermore, Senator William J. Fulbright of Arkansas called for new hearings on the course of the war in the Foreign Relations Committee.

Mansfield

Meanwhile, a petition calling for a top-to-bottom review of the nation's Vietnam policy received nearly 150 signatures in the House. More ominously for the president, Senator Robert

Kennedy of New York was determined to take Tet as an opportunity to break with the administration over the conduct of the war. To Johnson, always both paranoid and resentful of the Kennedy family, this was rank betrayal.

Bobby Kennedy

The most immediately significant of the newly empowered anti-war Democrats, however, was Minnesota Senator Eugene McCarthy. McCarthy, who had been considered as a possible running mate for Johnson in 1964, had grown increasingly skeptical of the war effort, and, on November 30, 1967, he declared that "there comes a time when an honorable man simply has to raise the flag," McCarthy officially announced that he would challenge Johnson for Democratic Party's nomination for president in 1968.

Initially, it seemed that McCarthy's low name recognition and controversial anti-war platform would doom his candidacy. On March 12, however, with reports of Westmoreland's request for additional troops still ricocheting through the news media, McCarthy came surprisingly close to defeating the president in the New Hampshire primary. In retrospect, this result probably overstates the extent of anti-war sentiment in New Hampshire; President Johnson, who had not yet decided whether to seek his party's nomination, did not appear on the ballot, yet he still managed to secure 49% of the vote as a write-in candidate. Further, polls showed that a good many McCarthy voters actually supported taking stronger measures in Vietnam and apparently viewed the senator as little more than a protest candidate.

Even so, both historians and observers at the time have interpreted the New Hampshire results as evidence that the Vietnam War, and particularly the Tet Offensive, had crippled the Johnson presidency. In McCarthy's own words, "It's curious about Tet. They still say it was a victory. [Secretary of State Dean] Rusk said we decided to ease up on the bombing because we'd won this great victory. And I guess technically they had, but you know the cost. And I sort of understood Rusk and Lyndon better when I read that they thought not just that they had won technically, but that this would be understood in the country as a great victory—just the numbers that were killed. They said, the kill ratio in Tet was twelve to three or twelve to two. But Americans didn't care how many Vietnamese were killed. It was just about then that Life magazine ran pictures of all the American servicemen killed in one week. It was when it got to the point where they were reporting [American casualties] in the county seat newspapers and everyone began to know the people who were being killed, that I sensed something political was happening." (McCarthy in Willenson, 85).

McCarthy

Thus, as Johnson was due to start his reelection campaign, the Democratic Party had divided deeply. The Party divided into roughly four groups, some of which deeply despised the other factions. Johnson and his Vice President, Hubert Humphrey, were supported by labor unions and party bosses – what might be called the "party establishment." McCarthy attracted support primarily from white students who opposed the Vietnam War. Bobby Kennedy was popular among Catholics and minority voters, including African-Americans and Hispanics. A fourth group, Southern segregationists, was threatening to bolt the Democratic Party altogether, and they tossed their support behind George C. Wallace of Alabama, who eventually decided to run for President without the Democratic Party's support.

"Hey, hey, LBJ, how many kids did you kill today?" became a rallying cry against the incumbent President, whose Vietnam policies were increasingly weighing down his hold on the White House. Four days after his razor-slim victory in New Hampshire, Johnson's arch political nemesis, Kennedy, announced his candidacy from the same location where his brother had announced his own eight years earlier: the Russell Senate Office Building in Washington. The McCarthy campaign charged that he was an opportunist, relying on McCarthy's initial candidacy before declaring its own, but regardless, the Kennedy name continued to attract Americans across the country, and Bobby seemed to represent another chance at Camelot.

Kennedy's candidacy, as well as McCarthy's, indicated the deep division within the Democratic Party over the Vietnam War. On the one side was President Johnson, while Kennedy and McCarthy together split the anti-war vote. Johnson was consumed by the Vietnam War while in the White House and had little time to campaign; in fact, he never left the White House during the New Hampshire campaign, and he feared that a long and brutal primary campaign, along with an equally onerous general election campaign, would sink his presidency and his chances of winning.

After New Hampshire, Johnson began to harbor second thoughts about running in 1968, and in late March, facing dissention on all sides, President Johnson convened a meeting of former diplomats, military officers, and government officials—the so-called "Wise Men"—to review the nation's Vietnam policy. Following two days of top-secret briefings, the group arrived at a dramatic consensus: the president should reverse course, refuse the military's request for reinforcements, halt all bombing of North Vietnam, and enter into talks for a negotiated settlement with the Communists. Given the fact that a good many of the "Wise Men" had been instrumental in designing the nation's disastrous war policy (the group included former generals Maxwell Taylor, Omar Bradley, and Matthew Ridgeway, as well as former secretary of state Dean Acheson, former national security advisor McGeorge Bundy, and former ambassador to South Vietnam Henry Cabot Lodge), Johnson was understandably apoplectic at their sudden about-face. The president reportedly complained, "The establishment bastards have bailed out."

Boxed in, and with erstwhile allies turning against him daily, Johnson acceded to the seemingly inevitable on March 31. Appearing on live television, he announced, "With America's sons in the fields far away, with America's future under challenge right here at home, with our hopes and the world's hopes for peace in the balance every day, I do not believe that I should devote an hour or a day of my time to any personal partisan causes or to any duties other than the awesome duties of this office—the presidency of your country. I shall not seek, and I will not accept, the nomination of my party for another term as your president." (Johnson, 1:469-76). With that, Giap's Tet Offensive claimed its greatest scalp.

The Vietnam War, of course, would continue to drag on for many more years to come, consuming both lives and livelihoods on all sides. Neither of Johnson's anti-war challengers would ultimately win the presidency; Robert Kennedy, who might conceivably have secured the Democratic Party's nomination, was assassinated on June 6 of that year, and Eugene McCarthy, despite enthusiastic backing from young anti-war Democrats, failed to secure the necessary support of party elites. Hubert Humphrey, Johnson's Vice President and the establishment candidate, would go on to lose the tightly contested 1968 election to Richard M. Nixon.

Nixon, convinced that further casualties on the scale of Tet would sink his administration as surely as they had sunk Johnson's, adopted a policy of "Vietnamization," gradually withdrawing American combat troops and replacing them with resources and training to enhance the size and effectiveness of South Vietnam's military. In the short term, this policy was reasonably successful; even as American troop numbers in Vietnam declined, the SVA (with large-scale American air support) managed to turn back a North Vietnamese offensive in 1972, and in 1973, the conclusion of the Paris Peace Accords produced a case-fire between North and South, setting the stage for the final withdrawal of all American forces in South Vietnam.

In the longer term, however, as both Nixon and National Security Advisor (later Secretary of State) Henry Kissinger well understood, the peace deal simply created a "decent interval" between American withdrawal and Communist victory. In April 1975, a final NVA offensive captured Saigon, and the Vietnam War was finally over.

Online Resources

Other books about Vietnam by Charles River Editors

Other books about the Tet Offensive on Amazon

Bibliography

Appy, Christian G., *Patriots: The Vietnam War Remembered from All Sides*, 2003

Arnold, James R., *Tet Offensive 1968: Turning Point in Vietnam*, 1990.

Braestrup, Peter, *Big Story: How the American Press and Television Reported and Interpreted the Crisis of Tet in Vietnam and Washington*, 1977.

Caputo, Philip, *A Rumor of War*, 1988.

Currey, Cecil, *Victory at Any Cost: The Genius of Viet Nam's Gen. Vo Nguyen Giap*, 1999.

Davidson, Phillip B., *Vietnam at War*, 1988.

Dougan, Clark and Stephen Weiss, *The Vietnam Experience: Nineteen Sixty-Eight*, 1983.

Duiker, William J., *The Communist Road to Power in Vietnam*, 1981.

Falk, Richard, *Appropriating Tet*, 1988.

Gilbert, Marc Jacob and William Head, eds., *The Tet Offensive*, 1996.

Johnson, Lyndon B., *Public Papers of the Presidents of the United States: Lyndon B. Johnson, 1968-69*, 1970.

Karnow, Stanley, *Vietnam: A History*, 2nd ed., 1997

Lawrence, Margaret Atwood, *The Vietnam War: A Concise International History*, 2008.

Moss, George Donelson, *A Vietnam Reader: Sources and Essays*, 1991.

Murphy, Edward F., *Semper Fi Vietnam: From Da Nang to the DMZ, Marine Corps Dampaigns , 1965-1975*, 1997.

Oberdorfer, Don, *Tet! The Turning Point in the Vietnam War*, 2001.

Olson, James S. and Randy Roberts, *Where the Domino Fell: America and Vietnam, 1945 to 1990*, 1991.

Shulimson, Jack et al, *US Marines in Vietnam: The Defining Year 1968*, 1997.

Summers, Harry, *Historical Atlas of the Vietnam War*, 1995.

Summers, Col. Harry G., *On Strategy: A Critical Analysis of the Vietnam War*, 1984.

Tran Van Tra, *Vietnam: History of the Bulwark B2 Theater, Volume 5: Concluding the 30-Years War, Southeast Asia Report No. 1247*, 1983.

Vandiver, Frank E., *Shadows of Vietnam*, 1997.

Werner, Jayne S. and Luu Doan Huynh, eds., *The Vietnam war: Vietnamese and American Perspectives*, 1993.

Westmoreland, William C., *A Soldier Reports*, 1976.

Willbanks, James H., *The Tet Offensive: a Concise History*, 2007.

Willenson, Kim, *The Bad War: an Oral History of the Vietnam War*, 1987.

Young, Marilyn B. *The Vietnam Wars, 1945 – 1990*, 1990.

Made in the USA
Columbia, SC
13 May 2022

60390911R00041